## A SPECIAL MESSAGE JUST FOR YOU

## THIS BOOK IS LOANED TO YOU BY:

_____

_____

_____

## RETURN IT OR PAY IT FORWARD.

# ——— THE ———
# FOUR YEAR
## CAREER®

How to Make Your Dreams of Fun
& Freedom Come True

or Not...

## THE MASTERS EDITION

# RICHARD BLISS BROOKE

ISBN # 978-0-9979206-8-0
Published by Bliss Business, LLC
418 East Lakeside Avenue, Suite 121
Coeur d'Alene, Idaho 83814
P: 855.480.3585
Printed in the United States of America

# RICHARD BLISS BROOKE

In 1977, Richard was working at Foster Farms, the single largest chicken processing plant in the world. With 40 years to go until retirement, he decided to change course; and at the age of 22, he joined the ranks of the Network Marketing profession.

Like it is for many people, Richard's first few years were a struggle. Then he figured something out—and three years later, he had **30,000 active partners building** the business with him. By the age of 28, he was **earning $40,000 a month**.

In 2017, had he stuck it out, Richard would have been retiring from Foster Farms. That's not a bad thing, just different.

In March 1992, *SUCCESS* magazine featured the Network Marketing industry's skyrocketing success as its lead story. It was the first time a mainstream publication had done so in the industry's 50-year history. That is your favorite chicken chopper turned CEO, Richard Bliss Brooke, in the middle picture. It outsold every issue in the 100-year history of the magazine.

Richard has been a **full-time Network Marketing professional since 1977**. He is a former member of the Board of Directors of the Direct Selling Association, a former senior member of the DSA Ethics Committee, as well as:

- Author of *The Four Year Career*® and *Mach2: The Art of Vision & Self-Motivation,* and host of the *Network Marketing Heroes* podcast
- Owner of a Network Marketing company for 30 years (sold in 2017)
- Industry Expert and Advocate
- Motivational Seminar Leader
- Ontological Coach
- Owner of BlissBusiness.com

Richard loves golf, Harleys, poker, boating, scuba diving, and ATVs. Mostly he loves his wife, Kimmy. The Brookes live in Lanai, Hawaii, and Coeur d'Alene, Idaho.

Richard's own personal story is certainly exceptional and is not what the average person chooses to achieve or is capable of achieving in the business. Network Marketing is not for everyone … perhaps not even for most people. And those who do choose to pursue it usually lose interest in the income option. Building a sales organization takes time, usually years, and most people do not stick with it.

Fortunately, when the products are excellent, even those people who give up on the income option may choose to keep using the products and recommending them when it is convenient. These are the people who make up most of the *"sales force and sales volume."*

At the end of the day, a person can figure out how something won't work or figure out how it will. Either way, each attitude is a self-fulfilling prophecy.

---

"It is in the nature of revolution, the overturning of an existing order, that at its inception a very small number of people are involved. The process, in fact, begins with one person and an idea, an idea that persuades a second, then a third and a fourth, and gathers force until the idea is successfully contradicted, absorbed into conventional wisdom, or actually turns the world upside down. A revolution requires not only ammunition, but also weapons and men willing to use them and willing to be slain in the battle. In an intellectual revolution, there must be ideas and advocates willing to challenge an entire profession, the establishment itself, willing to spend their reputations and careers in spreading the idea through deeds as well as words."

— JUDE WANNISKI, 1936-2005
*The Way the World Works* (Touchstone Books, 1978)

All examples in this book are hypotheticals. Remember: only 5% of Network Marketers attempt to build an Asset Income and less than 1% build anything of substance. The only income possibilities you should rely on are those contained in a particular company's "Income Disclosure Statement." If a copy of it is not included with this book, ask for it. It will give you the annual income averages at all levels.

# Connect with Richard Online

FACEBOOK.COM/RICHARDBLISSBROOKE

INSTAGRAM.COM/RICHARDBLISSBROOKE

YOUTUBE.COM/USER/RBBROOKE

LINKEDIN.COM/IN/RICHARDBLISSBROOKE

RICHARDBROOKE.COM

# TABLE OF CONTENTS

**Laura Evans, Doug & Charlene Fike, Laura Hostetler,
Barb & Ray Madorin, Roland Oosterhouse
Chris & Jessica Page, Gene & Nedra Sahr, DeDe Shaw,
Marty & Sheryl Turner, Carolyn Wightman**

# A PERSONAL NOTE

The sales leaders featured in the back of this book all chose to build their empires in one particular company. Because we do not have permission, I won't name that company, but the person who gave you this book is probably marketing their products.

I first tried their products in 1977 ... my first year in Network Marketing ... in fact, the same week I launched my Network Marketing business in a different company. The company I chose made a lot of flashy promises. I bought their promises.

Had I been wiser and more experienced, I would have chosen to build in this company ... the one these leaders chose. Why? Because the company I unfortunately chose went out of business in 12 years after I had spent 9 years building my empire; it was heartbreaking and very expensive.

Decades later, I had the opportunity to spend time with the current owner of the company in this book: a true Renaissance Man with a crystal-clear vision and the resources to lead this company to be one of, if not *the* most successful, respected, and admired Network Marketing companies in the world.

This company has proven itself for over 60 years to provide immensely valuable products and a culture of ethical opportunity that has resulted in extraordinary wealth and freedom for those who had the vision and courage to build it.

I offered to create this edition of *The Four Year Career®* featuring some of the most successful sales leaders in the company because I believe in the integrity, products, mission, values, and wealth-building opportunities this company provides.

Only you can decide if they are for you. But this I can promise: this company will not let you down. They will not embarrass you. They will inspire you with their cutting-edge, scientifically proven products and a destiny that will bring chills.

I am not part of this company. I just admire it.

*Bill B. Brooks*

# PREFACE

"When Galileo invited scholars to look through his telescope in order to see the new evidence, they flatly refused. They didn't want to see any data that might count against the earth-centric view of the universe. It is difficult to think of a more revelatory episode of cognitive dissonance. They simply shut their eyes."

— MATTHEW SYED
*Black Box Thinking: Why Most People Never Learn from Their Mistakes–But Some Do* (Portfolio, 2015)

This book is intended to be a fair and honest view of Network Marketing. By writing this book, I clearly **endorse the Network Marketing** business model, but I am also one of its most **vocal critics** and **change agents.**

Since 1977, I have seen thousands of companies come and go ... just like in any other industry or profession. So when a company tells us they are going to be *"the next big thing,"* it means nothing. Promises are easy to make. **Execution over decades is the only thing that demonstrates integrity and competency.**

Primarily, the reputation of the profession has been **created by the hype** ... the empty promises and manipulation toward making a lot of income quickly for not a lot of effort ... and a deception about what the financial option is all about.

For decades, prospects would ask if what the sales reps were talking about was Network or Multi-level Marketing, and the sales reps would go to great lengths to convince them it was not. It was NOT like that company everyone had heard about. **And yet it was.**

*Some companies still promote this deception; they are clearly and factually a Network Marketing business model, yet they insist they are not. Social selling and leverage selling are just new, fancy names for Network Marketing.*

Over 70 years of deception and empty promises have created a reputation of distrust. We earned it. And it is left to us to change it.

I have also seen that, for those people who *"figure it out,"* their lives are forever enriched financially, physically, emotionally, and spiritually by the **journey of Network Marketing**.

Some would say that it's not fair that only a few people create the success they want in Network Marketing. I would say that everyone who *"takes a look"* at Network Marketing as a part-time income or significant wealth-building alternative has the **same option to succeed**. Life is not fair if you define fairness as *"everyone wins."* My mentors never promised me life would be fair. They just promised me it would *"be."* **The rest was up to me.**

In reading this book, you'll learn how and why our business model works ... **when you actually do the work**.

Our model is challenging. Most companies go out of business. Most products are not really viable, high-demand products outside of the financial option. And most people you ask to join will say no. Perhaps the most challenging part is that during the period of the

Four Year Career when you put in the most work, you get paid the least. This is **not an immediate gratification option**. Most of the income is delayed … often for years.

In the first year or two, you may not earn an exciting income based on the work done. Your income is more linear, meaning **you earn in direct proportion to the results YOU create**.

If you are successful at building a team, this linear period is short in comparison to the second phase of income … the compounded or residual phase. These are the years that **your income is compounded by the teammates** who are doing what you did in the beginning … growing their own teams. The compounding phase can last decades, even a lifetime.

The comparison of the timeline is remarkable: **the tough building phase vs. the compounding phase**. Those who succeed keep their eyes on the compounding phase to motivate through the build.

The challenge with people succeeding is not their character or work ethic. It is purely their motivation.

**Motivation is the story we tell ourselves about whether or not the work is worth it.** If we have a story of doubt, frustration, fear, or even a story of how we *"don't want to bother our friends,"* then we are more motivated to avoid doing the work than doing it. One intention of this book is to help you **craft your own story** about Network Marketing. Maybe the perspectives and facts herein will help you see the business—and yourself—differently.

# Possibilities

Our profession is often criticized and censored for telling our stories and showing what is possible. This book is not about claiming what will happen for you, but rather giving you enough information to **decide for yourself what is possible**.

Success in Network Marketing requires the same types of talents, efforts, and commitments required to succeed in any business. **There is no free lunch here** … because freedom is not free.

---

JUST AS WE WOULD ENCOURAGE A CHILD TO PURSUE HIS OR HER DREAMS, WE DO NOT SHY AWAY FROM ENCOURAGING THOSE WHO ARE INTERESTED. ONLY ONE IN TENS OF MILLIONS WILL EVER WIN AN OLYMPIC GOLD MEDAL. LESS THAN 5 PERCENT OF NEW REALTORS WILL EVER SELL A HOME. BUT HOW DO WE KNOW WHICH ONES WILL?

THAT'S WHY WE ENCOURAGE EVERYONE WITH A VISION AND AMBITION FOR A BETTER LIFE TO PURSUE IT WITH PASSION. IT IS WORTH IT TO US TO ENCOURAGE EVERYONE SO THAT A FEW CAN ACHIEVE THEIR DREAMS.

---

# THE 40/40/40 PLAN

"YOU CAN EITHER BE BUILDING YOUR IDEAL LIFE OR WORKING TO BUILD SOMEONE ELSE'S. SOMEONE'S DREAM IS BEING BUILT EITHER WAY."

— Richard Bliss Brooke

Since the dawn of the Industrial Revolution, over 250 years ago, the idea of a career has been to work (at least) 40 hours a week for 40 years for 40% of what was never enough for the first 40 years.

# The 40/40/40 Plan

The mandated path for most of us has been:

1. **Get a good education** … a four-year degree is your ticket.

2. **Get a good job** with a big company … with lots of benefits.

3. **Work for 40 years to retire** and enjoy the golden years.

Things have changed a lot since then. Your company is more likely to file bankruptcy to avoid paying your retirement than it is to honor it.

Even states, counties, and cities are starting to face the fact that they overpromised and can't deliver, and are filing bankruptcy to ditch their retirement and health care obligations. And even if the retirement is there … even a 401k … there is **rarely enough income** from this model to have a grand ol' time in your golden years.

> ## MOST PEOPLE JUST HUNKER DOWN AND RUN OUT THE CLOCK. I DON'T KNOW; MAYBE THEY THINK THIS IS A TRIAL RUN AND THEY'LL GET ANOTHER SHOT AT IT.

And what about that four-year degree? Most young adults following the college model do end up **well trained to get a job but are also well saddled with debt.** This debt cannot be discharged in bankruptcy, it can rarely be renegotiated, and most people are ill-afforded to pay it off. Since most people in their 30s and 40s are not even working in the careers they majored in, the debt they are carrying is a depressing load.

**Note:** I am not advocating against education or a job. I believe both are immensely valuable and rewarding. I am advocating against believing that just because you have both, you will live the life you really want … like you are on autopilot for the success you imagine.

**The cheese has been moved.[1] There is a piece of it over in Network Marketing.**

---

1 *Who Moved My Cheese?* by Spencer Johnson

# WHAT EXACTLY IS IT?

"BUILD IT ONCE ... EARN ON IT FOREVER ... IF DONE RIGHT"

— Richard Bliss Brooke

What is Network Marketing?

First, here is what Network Marketing is NOT:

## Retail Chain or Brick and Mortar Business.

There is NO income option for others involved, just straight transactions and income for the owner.

## Franchising.

Here, you are basically buying a full-time job. Your chances of success are very good if you have $25,000 to $2,500,000 and are willing to go all in, including working 60-70 hours a week.

## Affiliate Marketing.

You promote a link to a product and earn a small commission on your sales. The distinction is that you only earn income on the customers you personally refer. Also, you may or may not love the product and use it yourself.

## Internet Marketing.

You market a product online by building platforms, pages, and funnels. You earn on your sales. You may or may not love the product and use it yourself.

## Traditional Direct Sales.

This is the original form of sales and business and has been around for thousands of years. You get hired to sell a product directly to the public, either to leads provided by the company or through your own prospects. You earn only on your sales. You may or may not love the product and use it yourself. There is an option in Direct Sales to build a team. Sometimes you can build one without being "promoted" to do so. Sometimes you have to wait until someone promotes you. In either case, you will only earn a commission on the people you recruit to sell … a one-level option.

There are, of course, many variations of the above.

# What Network Marketing IS

Network Marketing is a form of direct selling that's also referred to as Multi-level Marketing. **It is done personally face-to-face**; via the **Internet** and **social media**; and through **trade shows, direct mail**, and **owner-operated businesses**, such as healthcare and beauty providers and nutritional outlets.

Occasionally, the classic pyramid scheme masquerades as a Network Marketing company. The differences are clear and easy to discern, and the guidelines are detailed later in the book.

The Network Marketing profession now produces **over $35.5 billion in annual sales by 20.5 million people in the U.S.** $182.5 billion worth of goods and services are sold worldwide each year in the industry, and there are more than 147 million people around the world who participate at some level in this concept.

——————————————

NETWORK MARKETING IS DEFINED BY THE RULE THAT EVERYONE MAY ENROLL OTHERS FROM DAY ONE. EVERYONE. FROM DAY ONE.

——————————————

This can create a **compounded growth** of the sales organization when it is followed. Most members do not take advantage of it, but those who do can grow a sales force.

Individual members may individually sell a lot of product or just use the products themselves and sell little or none. A really important number to ask about any particular option is … what is the average usage/sales per member? In the more successful companies, that number is **$400–$500 each**.

This contrasts with a more traditional direct sales model where the emphasis is on how much each sales rep sells, and this is influenced by high quotas.

For example, if a company in a traditional direct sales model wanted to sell **$500,000 a month of a product**, it might hire **500 excellent salespeople** and give them a protected territory. But the most important thing they would give them is the **quota of $1,000** a month in sales. 500 times $1,000 equals the $500,000 in sales.

In Network Marketing, we just flip the numbers via the rule that everyone may enroll others from day one. We compound our growth of sales reps looking to, for example, build a **team of 1,000**, each of whom may be **using/selling $500** a month. 1,000 times $500 equals $500,000.

More importantly, the team and their sales have the option to grow just by growing the sales force vs. trying to get each person to sell more. 1,000 people on the team can grow to 2,000 by **each member just enrolling one more** on their team.

The entire process is slowed by the historical fact that **less than 5% of people who enroll ever enroll anyone else**, and just choose to use and sell the products to others.

ANOTHER WAY OF EXPLAINING NETWORK MARKETING IS ...
"A LOT OF PEOPLE DOING A LITTLE BIT EACH."

One          vs.          Many

THE DIFFERENCES BETWEEN SALESPEOPLE AND
NETWORK MARKETING PEOPLE ARE:

| SALES | | NETWORK MARKETING |
|---|---|---|
| Full-time | vs. | Some-time |
| Salespeople | vs. | Customers |
| Employees | vs. | Volunteers |
| Quotas | vs. | Incentives |
| Protected Territories | vs. | No Territories |

## To Sell $500,000:

| 500 salespeople each sell $1,000 = $500,000 | vs. | 1,000 volunteers each sell $500 = $500,000 |
|---|---|---|

# Swapping the Numbers:
# A Big Paradigm Shift

Most of us grew up with a traditional selling paradigm. It sounds like this … if you have the option to earn money with a product, what you are supposed to do is sell a lot of product. **The more you sell, the more money you earn. Right?**

Instead of professional salespeople with quotas, **Network Marketing is based on satisfied customers**. Most of them do not like to sell but are happy to tell others about the products they use. These customers are not full-time or part-time employees. They are independent volunteers with no quotas and no protected territories. They "work" because they are **raving fans** of the products.

Network Marketing is not about personally selling a lot of product, although some distributors do. It is about **using and recommending the product** and, IF you see and believe in the wealth-building model, finding a lot of others to do the same.

# ATTRIBUTES THAT DEFINE NETWORK MARKETING

1. **You LOVE the product** and promote it based on your own authentic and passionate story.

2. **You promote the product** to people (both those you already know and those you don't) by networking.

3. **Everyone, from day one, can build a team**. Everyone. From day one.

4. **Building a team creates the potential for geometric growth**. Think family generations.

5. **You potentially get paid on ALL the sales** of all generations of the team. It's like you're the great-great-great-grandmother, and you get paid on all the sales of your family tree.

Keep in mind that building a sales team is a lot harder than it looks on paper. Fewer than **5% who attempt to build** any size team actually do it, and the percentage of people who build one into the hundreds is single digits. The percentage of people who build a team into the thousands is less than 1%.

Although the odds of building any kind of wealth are slim, that does not deter people from going for it. Why not? There is **little to lose** as long as you are smart with your money … and a **great deal to gain**. In the end, most people (90%) who join any Network Marketing company just do so because they love the products and the people.

# 3 Levels of Participation in Network Marketing

## Customers

Customers are people who fall in love with the product and **buy it for their own use**. Contrary to some spin, the bar is higher for customers to buy from a Network Marketer. It is easier to lump buying anything into your regular visit to the store or your favorite online retailer. When a customer buys from a Network Marketer, they have to make a separate buying transaction. The **product has to be special** to warrant this.

The bar is even higher for repeat customer sales or *"auto ship,"* which a lot of customers prefer. For a customer to remain a repeat customer, they have to love the product so much that all the "advertising" they see on social media or anywhere else does not sway them to try something different. Network Marketers do not tend to bombard their customers with advertising but **prefer education and gratitude** as their tools to maintain customer loyalty.

## Distributors

Customers transition into distributors, members, consultants, ambassadors, etc. It happens when they not only love a product but are **willing to tell their stories to others** and potentially gather some customers of their own.

Distributors may sell directly to local customers out of inventory they carry, or they may just promote a link to a site where the customer can purchase.

Distributors generally approach *"selling"* very casually, and as a result, they earn a sporadic income at best. Some pursue their roles with **passion and purpose** and earn a nice income from their sales.

In most companies, 90% of all Network Marketing participants are either customers or distributors.

## Sales Leaders

Sales leaders have the **intention of building a team** of customers, distributors, and other sales leaders. *The Four Year Career®* was written about, and for, sales leaders: ambitious and courageous people who are committed to creating new adventures of freedom and fun in their lives.

This book is written for the 5 percenters ... those who are and those who may aspire to be. *The Four Year Career®* is not about Network Marketing as a whole. Rather, it's for the few who can see the value of building a beautiful team of people who share a love for a product and a network of "income centers" that span the globe.

# THE POWER OF NETWORK MARKETING

"YOU'RE NEVER TOO YOUNG TO START AN EMPIRE AND
YOU'RE NEVER TOO OLD TO INSPIRE ONE."

— Richard Bliss Brooke

There is a strategy that anyone can employ to build wealth, regardless of age, experience, education, income level, or social status:

**Asset Income from Network Marketing.**

# A Network Marketing Income Offers These Advantages

1. You can **build it part time**, anytime. You choose when and how. Building it "sometimes" does not work. But if you dedicate even just one hour a day … a specific hour set aside to build your team, you can make it work.

2. You can **build it from anywhere**: any city, any virtual office, any phone, tablet, or laptop.

3. You can **launch it for $500 to $1,000**. You may choose to spend more on education, tools, travel, etc., but you do not have to. It is possible to launch yourself right into profit by just getting some initial products and a sales kit.

4. You are **in business for yourself, but not by yourself**. This means your host company takes on the heavy lifting: investing in product development, legal groundwork, brand marketing, IT and back office support, administration of compensation and incentives, and customer service to sales leaders … their manufacturer's reps. In addition, they can collaborate with sales leaders on recognition and education, as well as consumer marketing and support.

5. Your business partners—those above you in the network in terms of seniority and lineage—have a **vested interest in your success**. Somewhere in your team, someone is making it work, and they want more than anything to teach and motivate you to make it work.

6. The **tax code** in most countries favors those who own a business ... any business, large or small. There are advantages waiting for you when you own a Network Marketing business. Talk to your accounting professional about what they are.

7. You can **learn it while you earn it**. You can create cash flow your first month. Although not everyone creates cash flow right away, and you may not even choose to strategically, it is possible. If you need immediate income, talk to your enroller and coaches about how you can maximize your income and minimize your expenses right away.

8. You can **create the wealth-building trifecta**. Earn the extra income you do not have now to invest in real estate and stocks. Most people do not have the extra income to invest in traditional wealth-building options. This can give you that option.

9. Your income can **keep pace with inflation** because the product sales on which you get paid will rise in price over time, just like everything else. Termite-proof your income!

10. **With time and success**, your income can be produced for you by hundreds, perhaps even thousands, of people, each pursuing their own success. This creates an Asset Income, meaning it could go on forever regardless of whether you are driving it or not. **A pure Asset Income creates an asset or net worth.**

**Note: All examples in this book are hypotheticals. Remember: only 5% of Network Marketers attempt to build an Asset Income and less than 1% build anything of substance. The only income possibilities you should rely on are those contained in a particular company's "Income Disclosure Statement." If a copy of it is not included with this book, ask for it. It will give you the annual income averages at all levels.**

# The #1 Benefit of Network Marketing Is the Ability to Build Asset Income

---

YOU BUILD SOMETHING ONCE THAT COULD PAY YOU FOREVER. IT IS LIKE AN INVENTION OR A SONG OR A BOOK ... OR A BUSINESS THAT RUNS ITSELF.

---

Asset Income from Network Marketing is the business that runs itself. *How can that be?*

It's not like any other business where you hire employees to run your business while you sit on the beach or golf. In this case, it runs itself by splitting up the income sources from hundreds or thousands of sources. This doesn't mean that what you do does not matter. Your role is more about recognition, inspiration, and guidance. **It is a leadership role versus a sales role.**

These sources are your sales leaders ... **leaders who have their own vision and ambition.** Leaders who are implementing a model that you implemented. At some point, they learn all they can from you and go out on their own. Sometimes this takes months, sometimes a few years. But when you are earning $50 a month from 50 different people, you have spread your risk out so far among so many independent business people, that what YOU are doing every month is the source of your income. They may actually be inspired that you are on the beach or golfing.

And, of course, you all have to be selling a product that is in high, long-term demand by consumers … people who will happily pay your price.

When your income comes to you each month like that you have Asset Income. In other words, **what you have built is an asset more than a business**. If your Network Marketing income is $2,500 a month in pure residuals/Asset Income, meaning what you do every month influences your team but is not the determining factor, then you could say your **asset is worth 200 times the income**, or in this case, $500,000. How is that? Because that is how much rental real estate or dividend-producing stocks you would need to own to earn $2,500 a month.

Can you sell your $2,500-a-month distributorship for $500,000? No. Because **any highly motivated person can build** one of their own in 2–3 years. Why would they pay you a lifetime of savings for something they could build themselves? But in terms of a wealth-building asset, it can be said that your income is worth 200 times the monthly income.

## What Does It Mean to "Retire on Your Asset Income"?

What you get paid for in Network Marketing *"retirement"* is your leadership … leadership of what you've built in the past and your current role in inspiring others. **Retired Network Marketing leaders have the most fun.** They get to celebrate others, take the best team trips, and watch their best leaders surpass their own achievements.

# Facts about Network Marketing

## Fact #1: It's legal.

In the U.S. and around the world in over **70 countries**, Network Marketing has been legally used for product distribution and distributor compensation for **more than 70 years**.

During this time, Network Marketing has repeatedly been upheld by the federal and state courts as a legal distribution and compensation method when the **following legal guidelines are followed**:

**A.** The main objective of the business is **selling viable products or services at a market-driven price**. Meaning, there is a market for the product from consumers absent of the financial option. The test is simple. Would you or do you have customers who are buying the product without any connection to the Network Marketing financial option? Is it a real product at a market-driven price or is the product a shill in a money game?

**B.** **Potential incomes aren't promised.** Even hypothetical incomes aren't inferred without the appropriate disclaimers. This is not an even playing field with the rest of the business world; even lotteries get to hype us into thinking we might win millions (even though we have better odds of getting struck by lightning).

Regardless of whether or not our profession is treated fairly, it is illegal for an option to promote how much some people earn or how much you can earn without prominently displaying what is called an Income Disclosure Statement. This statement shows you how much the average person earns and how long it takes them to earn it. If you do not see one of these full disclosure statements, ask for it.

C. Distributors are **not paid for the act of recruiting others** (headhunting fees). Income has to come entirely from the sale of products.

There are many products or services that distributors will be "customers" for as long as there is a financial option to go with it. The means justify the end. Unfortunately, when all the shine wears off, no one continues to use the product.

The true test of a **legitimate** Network Marketing company is whether most of the product is sold to consumers who are not earning commissions or royalties from the income option. Most Network Marketing distributors start out pursuing the income option, but once they give up, they settle in to being customers. Most companies' total sales are made up of these "wholesale" customers. Maybe they sell enough to get their product for free. This is easily 90% of most Network Marketing sales forces. They don't have any distributors on their teams. They are just using the product. They are customers.

## Fact #2: Most companies fail, some succeed.

There are an estimated **1,000 Network Marketing firms distributing over $35.5 billion a year** in goods and services in the U.S. alone.

Most Network Marketing companies do not succeed. Most restaurants do not. Most dry cleaners do not. Most companies we went to work for just out of college or high school have already failed. And some do succeed.

Herbalife, Mary Kay, Forever Living Products, Nu Skin, Amway,

Young Living, Arbonne, Shaklee, and Usana are billion-dollar brands and have been in business and growing steadily for 20 to 60 years. **Hundreds of other companies sell between $10 million and $1 billion a year through millions of independent brand representatives.**

This is the nature of free markets and enterprise.

### Fact #3: Most people who start out saying they want to build a team end up saying later that they do not.

Most people give up. Most people fail. This is not a *"most people succeed"* option like franchising. **It's all about motivation, priorities, and the marketplace.** As a factual basis, this cannot be overstated.

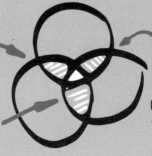

If 100 people say they are going to build a team:

1/3 WILL NEVER DO ANYTHING

1/3 WILL TRY AND THEN QUIT

1/3 WILL DO SOMETHING, EVEN IF IT'S JUST USING THE PRODUCTS AS A CUSTOMER

5% to 10% of the people you enroll will build a team ... some small, some big.

For those who *"do something,"* that does not mean they necessarily earn a profit themselves but that they create some customers and new team members. The thing is, we never know which people are going to end up in which category.

### Fact #4: We are a major player in the global economy, and we are growing!

The Network Marketing method of marketing as an industry has grown 19 out of the last 21 years, including over 92% in just the past 11 years. $182.5 billion worth of goods and services are sold worldwide each year in the industry, and there are more than 147 million people worldwide who participate at some level in this concept.

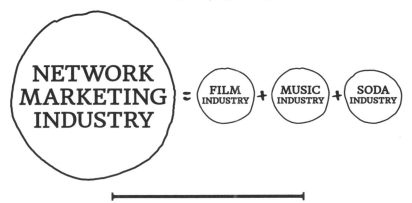

WORLDWIDE SALES FROM THE NETWORK MARKETING INDUSTRY ARE LARGER THAN GLOBAL FILM AND ENTERTAINMENT INDUSTRY SALES, GLOBAL MUSIC SALES, AND GLOBAL SALES FROM THE LEADING SOFT DRINK COMPANY ... COMBINED!

NETWORK MARKETING INDUSTRY ≈ ( FILM INDUSTRY ) + ( MUSIC INDUSTRY ) + ( SODA INDUSTRY )

# A FEW EXAMPLES OF THE 1,000 PLUS NETWORK MARKETING COMPANIES AROUND THE WORLD

| | |
|---|---|
| 4Life | Nu Skin |
| ACN | Plexus |
| AdvoCare | Pruvit |
| Ambit Energy | Purium |
| Arbonne International | Rodan + Fields |
| Asea | Scentsy |
| Doterra | SendOutCards |
| Forever Living | Shaklee |
| Isagenix | Optavia |
| Immunotec | Usana |
| Jeunesse Global | Utility Warehouse |
| Juice Plus+ | WorldVentures |
| Le-Vel | Yoli |
| LegalShield | Young Living |
| LifeVantage | Youngevity |
| Mannatech | Younique |
| Modere | Zurvita |

People who are drawn to Network Marketing are also drawn to people of influence: people who encourage change, growth, abundance, and risk. **Here's what some famous influencers say about the Network Marketing model …**

# It Works

**Tony Robbins**, American motivational speaker and author of *Unlimited Power, Unleash the Power Within* and *Awaken the Giant Within*

> "What's beautiful about Network Marketing is you get all the benefits of being a business owner, without all the headaches, and without the same level of risk. And so I think Network Marketing's amazing!"

**Richard Branson**, Founder of Virgin Group, business magnate, investor, and philanthropist

> "I'm a tremendous Believer in Network Marketing."

**Jim Rohn**, entrepreneur, author, and motivational speaker

> "Network Marketing is really the greatest source of grassroots capitalism, because it teaches people how to take a small bit of capital, that is our time, and build the American dream."

**Bob Proctor**, the "Foremost Personal Achievement Philosopher"

"What you sow, you reap. It's the law of nature. Network Marketing is perfectly aligned with that. You truly get EXACTLY what you are worth. NO nepotism, NO favoritism. That's rare today."

**Brian Tracy**, business coach, bestselling author, thought leader

"The future of Network Marketing is unlimited. There's no end in sight. It will continue to grow, because better people are getting into it. It will be one of the respected business methods in the world."

**Darren Hardy,** former publisher of *SUCCESS* magazine

"The future of employment is self-employment. Direct selling is one of the few business opportunities that offers average people, with above average ambition, to achieve an above average lifestyle, peace of mind, and financial security."

**Robert T. Kiyosaki**, author of *Rich Dad Poor Dad* and *The Business of the 21st Century*

"… Direct Selling gives people the option, with very low risk and very low financial commitment, to build their own income—generating assets and acquiring great wealth."

**Stephen Covey**, author of *The Seven Habits of Highly Effective People*

> "Network Marketing has come of age. It's undeniable that it has become a way to entrepreneurship and independence for millions of people."

**David Bach**, author of the *New York Times* bestseller *The Automatic Millionaire*

> "... you don't need to create a business plan or create a product. You only need to find a reputable company, one that you trust, that offers a product or service you believe in and can get passionate about."

**Tom Peters**, legendary management expert and author of *In Search of Excellence* and *The Circle of Innovation*

> "... the first truly revolutionary shift in marketing since the advent of 'modern' marketing at P&G and the Harvard Business School 50 to 75 years ago."

**Jim Collins**, author of *Built to Last* and *Good to Great*

> "... how the best organizations of the future might run – in the spirit of partnership and freedom, not ownership and control."

**Dave Ramsey,** *New York Times* bestselling author and radio host

"Multi-level Marketing, Network Marketing, and Direct Sales are the names used by those in that type of company to describe how their business models work. Their detractors call what they do 'one of those pyramid schemes' with a snarl. These companies are not pyramid schemes; they are a legitimate method for some people to make some side money and sometimes to literally build their own business."

**Warren Buffett,** billionaire investor and owner of three Direct Selling/Network Marketing companies

"The best investment Berkshire Hathaway ever made."

# THE POWER OF THE MYTHS

"THE WORST KIND OF ARROGANCE IS ARROGANCE FROM IGNORANCE."

— Richard Bliss Brooke

**M**yths are powerful forces. They are perpetuated by those who believe in them. All future *"evidence"* shows up as proof to further the myth (confirmation bias). Once we believe something, we work hard to sustain that belief ... to be right.

# Myth #1: Getting in on the ground floor is the best path to success in a Network Marketing company.

The truth is, it is the **worst time** to join. Most companies, including Network Marketing companies, go out of business in their first five years. Of course, no company is going to tell you that in their promotional materials. Everyone involved at the start of any company hopes it will succeed.

Another risk with a new company is that no company has its best foot forward early on. It takes **years to develop** competent, experienced staff, reliable procedures, and efficient services.

The best time to join a Network Marketing company is when it is **at least five to seven years old**. By then, it has demonstrated a commitment and ability to:

- Grow ethically
- Stay in business
- Honor its distributors and customers

And yet, this allows you the option to get involved with the company before they are so well-known that everyone has either already given them a try or decided they aren't interested.

Now, of course, if everyone adhered to this sage advice, none of us would be here. To the pioneers and courageous (the risk-takers) come both the thrill of victory and the agony of defeat. **The ground floor is not for the faint of heart.**

# Myth #2: Network Marketing is an option for someone who is not doing well financially to make some money—maybe even a lot of money.

Unfortunately, many of the success stories have perpetuated this myth with a rags-to-riches theme. Although there are enough people to substantiate the myth, it is still a myth.

The same **skills it takes to succeed** in any marketing business are required in Network Marketing:

- **You must have confidence**

- **You must be highly self-motivated**

- **You must be willing to market (talk, use social media, promote) to lots of people**

- **You must be consistent in your efforts**

- **You must stay after it until you succeed**

Your resources should include working capital, contacts, time, discipline, and a positive, crystal-clear vision of where you intend to go with your business—whether it is easy or not.

The truth is that many people who are struggling financially are doing so for a number of reasons, including low self-esteem and/or a lack of the basic skills and preparation that allow one to succeed in anything. Network Marketing is a powerful and dynamic economic model, but **not so powerful that it can overcome a person's lack of readiness or persistence**.

The people who are already successful in whatever they're doing now tend to also succeed in Network Marketing.

**Successful people are rarely in a profession where they can earn on the leverage of thousands of other people.** Real estate agents, teachers, coaches, medical professionals, counselors, small business owners, beauty professionals, and physical fitness professionals may be stellar performers in their domains, but how do they create the opportunity to earn on the efforts of thousands of others in their same professions? Here, they could.

# Myth #3: Network Marketers succeed by being in the right place at the right time.

Also not true. Timing and being in the right place all have to do with catching trends, fads, bull markets, and cycles. Wealth building in Network Marketing has nothing to do with all that. There are plenty of examples of people who have joined what may appear to be the most boring company—one that has millions of distributors already—and that person rises to the top. **Timing is a myth touted by promoters who are selling the sizzle.**

# Myth #4: The way Network Marketing works is the "big guys" make all their money off the "little guys."

The **"big guys, little guys"** myth is usually perpetuated by people who define fairness as *"everyone gets the same benefits, regardless of their contributions."* That is how socialism works, not how Network Marketing works.

In Network Marketing, the people who **attract**, **train**, and **motivate** the most salespeople earn the most money. Period.

If you end up with a little team, or no team at all, you'll still be on someone's team that is large. And they will earn a tiny little bit on your small efforts. If you don't like that, build a big team. Know that in doing so, you're building an even bigger team for that "Big Guy or Gal."

**That does not mean people with the bigger teams always earn more income.** If I enroll you, and only you, and you go on to build a huge team by enrolling many other successful sales leaders, you will always be on my team, and my team will always be bigger than yours. Yet you will earn far more income than I will. **Income is not tied directly to how many team members you have but how productive they are.**

Nor does timing have anything to do with income. Just because a person has been involved since the beginning does not mean they earn more money. The income in Network Marketing is tied to the number and productivity of the team you develop. There are many cases where a new team is developed in a legacy company, a company that has been around for decades, and the **new team leader earns far more** than those leaders who have been around for a long time.

**Here is an example:**

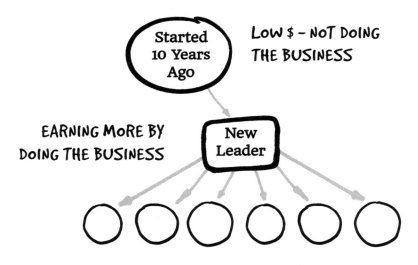

# Myth #5: You have to use your friends and family to make any money in Network Marketing.

The truth is, you do not, and you should not. Your friends and family should only become a part of your business if it serves them to do so. **If it serves them**—if they see an opportunity for themselves just like you did—then they are not being used; they are being served. If you do not believe your option can serve them, do not offer it to them.

An option that truly inspires you will most likely inspire them as well. Offer it to them. If they say no, respect and honor their viewpoint, and do not make a nuisance of yourself.

# Myth #6: If Network Marketing really worked, everyone would get involved and the market would be saturated.

Although this is mathematically possible, history has proven that saturation is not an issue. There are many companies mentioned in this book that have been in business for 30 to 50 years doing billions of dollars a year in business with millions of sales reps. Yet you are not one of them, nor are **298 million** people in the U.S. and **6.9 billion** people worldwide.

PLUS, YOU MIGHT CONSIDER A GREAT LEADER WHO PERSONALLY SPONSORED 12 PEOPLE 2,000 YEARS AGO. THEY HAVE ALL BEEN RECRUITING VIA WEEKLY MEETINGS AND ONE-ON-ONES FOR ALL OF THOSE 2,000 YEARS. AND YET MOST OF THE WORLD DOES NOT SUBSCRIBE TO THEIR PROGRAM.

# THE POWER of INVESTING

"THE BEST INVESTMENT IS A LEVERAGED ONE."
— Richard Bliss Brooke

W hen planning their financial futures, people generally follow one or more of these 3 strategies:

# 1. Liquid Investments/Equities

Most of us already have these kinds of investments to some extent. We take what we can or will out of our paychecks after paying taxes and all of our bills. If we are fortunate and/or frugal, we might end up with **10% to invest** ... perhaps $500 to $1,000 a month. For many people, it's just the opposite ... they are going into debt at a rate of $500 to $1,000 a month.

**Which group are you in?**
**Who do you know in the latter group?**
**What are their options for change?**

The save and invest system does work when we work it. We need to **invest consistently**, every month, and we need to invest in ways that produce at least an aggressive return over time, such as 7%. Any one of us who started doing this from our first working years would end up with a sizable nest egg.

We were told all of our lives to invest in *"blue-chip stocks,"* the companies that would be here forever. Many of us followed this advice. However, sometimes even the best fail. Remember Blockbuster, Kodak, Compaq, RadioShack, Circuit City, Enron, Pan Am, Tower Records, Polaroid, MCI WorldCom, Bear Stearns, Lehman Brothers, PaineWebber, Woolworths, Arthur Andersen, Adelphia, TWA, DeLorean Motor Co., etc.? I bet you couldn't find a financial advisor who would not have said these were all good investments. Fast-forward to 2018 and these companies are gone.

Take a close look at the compounding chart for a reality check. **Invest $500 a month at 7% from age 30 to 70, and you will have over $1.3 million.** That asset will pay you $84,000 a year for life at 7%. How much would you need to invest to end up with the same amount if you wait until you are 50?

In order to achieve the same cash value in only 20 years (starting at age 50 through age 70), your required monthly investment is nearly $2,500! And notice I used a 7% return. That is quite a generous assumption. What are you earning on your investments on average since you started investing? 2%, 7%, or 10%?

That $84,000 a year may sound good right now for retirement, but you **must factor in inflation**. Inflation is the insidious pest that destroys wealth like termites in a home. $84,000 a year in 2035 will be worth less than half that in buying power.

Now, guess how much you'd accumulate if you save the way most people do ... randomly and only when you can afford to? If you save that same **$500 a month EVERY OTHER MONTH, you'd only have $261,983 in 40 years**.

The difference is $1,058,079  * Compounded Monthly

## 2. Real Estate

Many of us gain most of our net worth through the payments we make over time on our own homes. **This works because we must pay someone for a place to live**; therefore, we are consistent with the investment. In higher-end markets and any waterfront communities, historically the return is much more than 7%. However, we have also seen market corrections that have dropped real estate values by up to 50%, even in those coveted California and Florida markets.

### The Challenge

For most people who consider the above two strategies, it is deciding what to invest in, and more importantly, **where to get the money to invest**. These strategies work great if you have the extra $1,000 a month to invest every month without fail for 25 years.

And unfortunately, the downturns in the markets rarely give notice. Those who even invest for a living are, for the most part, completely caught off guard. Those of us who invest as a necessity are caught in the landslide.

The question is not whether the markets will appreciate ... they always have long term. The question is **what will they be doing the year you want or need to cash out**?

☑ **Do you save and invest EVERY month?**

☑ **Are you going to cash out when your assets are UP?**

☑ **Are you going to outpace the termites?**

# 3. The HITS Approach

This is a common investment strategy that many people take when planning their economic futures: I like to call it the *"Head in The Sand"* (HITS) approach, also known as *"The Hope Strategy."*

> *I hope everything will work out.*
> *I hope Social Security will be enough.*
> *I hope Social Security will even be around.*
> *I hope I'll somehow have enough retirement income.*
> *I hope somehow my debts will be paid off.*
> *I hope the stock market keeps rising.*
> *I hope inflation doesn't tear down what I built up.*

We're so afraid of the answers, or of not being able to figure out the answers, that we live in the **Sands of Denial**.

It might help for you to go through what I call **The Financial Wake Up Call**.

---

You can listen to the whole thing at:
### http://www.takingalook.com

---

**But the essence of it is this set of calculations:**

- **What is your age now?**

- **When do you want to be financially secure? (retire or just be free.)**

- **How many years left until that time?**

- **What income do you want in retirement/ freedom?**

At a 5% rate of return, you will need $500,000 for every $2,000 a month in income.

---

Go here to find out how much Social Security income you will have: **https://www.ssa.gov/oact/quickcalc/index.html**

---

If your Social Security income is projected to be $2,000, you already have about **$500,000 in net worth**!

What is your **net worth right now**? (Cash, stocks, 401k, rental real estate equity, etc., and NET of any debt? Do not include your primary home. You need to live somewhere!)

For every $500,000 more in net worth you want, you will need to **save and invest $500 per month at 5% for 33 years**.

Whatever income you project for yourself, reduce it by 1.9% every year or about 16% every 10 years into the future to factor in inflation.

For example, $2,500 in Social Security income 20 years from now is only worth $1,750 in actual buying power.

**Which do you find more practical?**

Save and invest $500–$1,000 a month on top of what you are already doing for 20 more years OR …

- **Find a product you LOVE.**

- **Listen to people and tell them your story.**

- **Ask people who have the financial ambition to "just take a look" at Network Marketing.**

## ENTER THE FOUR YEAR CAREER

# THE FOUR CORNERSTONES OF THE FOUR YEAR CAREER

"GEOMETRIC PROGRESSION IS TO NETWORK MARKETING WHAT COMPOUNDING IS TO WEALTH BUILDING."

— Richard Bliss Brooke

# The Four Year Career Option

The Four Year Career was originally conceived in 1977. Although I never went to college, I was working with a few college kids on building their Network Marketing businesses. I was living in Des Moines, Iowa, so I decided to **interview some marketing students at Drake University** to understand the effort and cost they were investing for four years of college in relation to the outcome.

---

**WHAT I WAS THINKING ABOUT WAS HOW SUCCESSFUL SOMEONE COULD BE IF THEY INVESTED SOME OF THEIR EFFORT AND STUDYING HOURS INTO BUILDING A NETWORK.**

---

I knew if someone invested even a fraction of the capital (in training, travel, tools, marketing, etc.) and a fraction of the time, that instead of graduating with debt and begging for a job, they could—not necessarily would—graduate with a residual income.

What kind of job would they end up accepting, what kind of posture would they have in looking for a job, where would they choose to live if they graduated with freedom? **I expect their choices and the story of their lives would be a lot different.**

Ultimately, I found that college kids were not the best candidates for this kind of career … too many distractions.

## So, THE FOUR YEAR CAREER BECAME A BUSINESS PLAN FOR PEOPLE WHO WERE READY FOR A CHANGE.

A change in their lifestyles, financial situations, and professional development; those ready to **break out of the 40/40/40 plan** and find freedom, faster.

Keep in mind, the "four years" is arbitrary. There is no magic number of years. I have seen people get free in less than a year's worth of effort while others take 6–7 years. And, of course, **most people never follow the plan** and end up right back in their old lives. That's not a bad thing. We all have it pretty good regardless of our chosen career paths.

Below is a model of The Four Year Career. Each person represented is a sales leader.

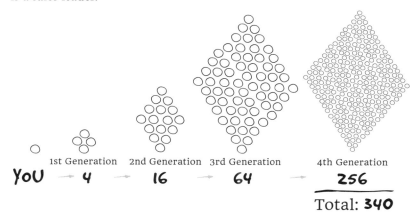

YoU → 4 → 16 → 64 → 256

1st Generation  2nd Generation  3rd Generation  4th Generation

Total: **340**

**You enroll 4 (who each enroll 4)
for 16 (who each enroll 4)
for 64 (who each enroll 4) for 256
for a total of 340 sales leaders.**

Keep in mind, this is just a model. No one in the history of Network Marketing has ever built a team of 4–16–64–256. It is dramatically more random than that. Some will enroll 1. Some will enroll 12. A few will enroll perhaps 100 over time. Think of it as a family tree. How many children each person in your family has is random, but by having children, the tree grows.

Each of you uses and recommends just an average of $200 a month in products for $68,000 in monthly sales, earning an average of 7% on each generation of sales for an Asset Income of $4,760 a month.

> Note: All examples in this book are hypotheticals. Remember: only 5% of Network Marketers attempt to build an Asset Income and less than 1% build anything of substance. The only income possibilities you should rely on are those contained in a particular company's "Income Disclosure Statement." If a copy of it is not included with this book, ask for it. It will give you the annual income averages at all levels.

## THE FOUR CORNERSTONES OF THE FOUR YEAR CAREER:

1. The People
2. The Product Sales
3. The Asset Income
4. The Asset Value

# The People

Remember … Network Marketing IS a lot of people doing a little bit *EACH*.

So how do we get 340 or even upwards of 1,000 people?

Two laws allow us to do it. The first was written by the creators for the Network Marketing concept who said, in essence: **"Anyone can, and should, enroll others."** This leads to the second law: **Geometric Progression**.

---

## "YOU ARE A NETWORK MARKETER. YOU OPERATE THE EIGHTH WONDER OF THE WORLD … GEOMETRIC PROGRESSIONS, ALSO KNOWN AS COMPOUNDING."

— Richard Bliss Brooke

---

So the question is: how do you get 1,000 people to be *"recommending for you"*?

**The answer is simple: you don't. You just get four, and then lead them to do the same.**

The path to gathering 1,000 people or more to *"sell for you"* in Network Marketing is Geometric Progression, which is made possible by the first Law in Network Marketing … that everyone, regardless of rank or time involved, is encouraged to invite and enroll others.

If you have been involved for one day you are encouraged to invite and enroll others. **This is the same if you have been involved for 10 years and are earning $10,000 a month.** Everyone enrolls new sales representatives. This creates the compounding impact.

You enroll four who each enroll four who each enroll four, etc.

**1 – 4 – 16 – 64 – 256 – 1,024 and so on.**

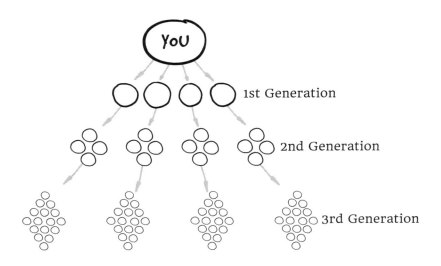

Note: All examples in this book are hypotheticals. Remember: only 5% of Network Marketers attempt to build an Asset Income and less than 1% build anything of substance. The only income possibilities you should rely on are those contained in a particular company's "Income Disclosure Statement." If a copy of it is not included with this book, ask for it. It will give you the annual income averages at all levels.

## It's Not Nearly as Easy as It Appears on Paper

This progression can quickly be overwhelming. But your role in Network Marketing is just to get the first four—not the whole bunch. **Focus your attention on just the first four.** And in actuality, you may build in units of two or three depending on your particular compensation model ... the same concept holds true.

The key to understanding the geometric option lies in a simple question:

*"If you really, really wanted to, could you find four people, anywhere in North America, to do this?"*

Before you answer, let's define *"do this."*

## "Doing This" ... Being a Sales Leader (aka Building a Four Year Career) Requires These 3 Activities:

### 1. Love and use the product.

This is a product you would use (at the price charged) forever; a product that gives you an experience that's so amazing you'd be compelled to talk about it whether you got paid to or not.

### 2. Recommend the product to others who are in need/want.

This can be done in person, in a group setting, via social media, or online. The best way to sell the product is to just listen to others, ask questions, listen some more, and if they give you the opportunity, tell them your product story. It is OK if they do not buy.

## 3. Invite customers and would-be customers to "just take a look" at the option.

You build a team by recruiting other sales leaders. And people look at the option because they want or need more income. So you are also selling an income option ... just by telling your story. Having people "take a look" can also be done with a simple video or by loaning them this book.

So I ask you again: **If you really, really wanted to, could you find four people in the next four to six months?**

Now, if you are not sure, what if I told you I would give you $500 for each of them ... $2,000 cash if you could get four in the next four months. Then could you? **Would you?**

Most people would answer yes. The reason is, if they really wanted to, anything like this is doable. Getting four people to earn more income is not THAT hard to do.

## IF YOU ANSWERED YES ...

Lock in on that YES; it is the key to believing you can get 1,000. Why? Because if you believe you will get four ... and they are four who are *"doing it"* ... then they will also be facing the same question.

Will they get four? If you are not sure ... ask them. And what is usually the result of someone really, really wanting to do something, and more importantly, believing they will do it, and being in action doing it? **It eventually gets done.**

Now remember, I am typing this on my laptop. Creating it in actual, real-life human production requires more than just simple keystrokes.

Perhaps you are *"getting it"* right now. Perhaps you need to let it rest or doodle it on a notepad …

$$1-2-4-8$$
$$1-3-9-27$$
$$1-4-16-64$$
$$1-5-25-125$$

This is how Geometric Progression will work for you. One person each believing they will get four creates … You – 4 – 16 – 64 – 256 – 1,024 – 4096 and so on.

The secret module is that 1 – 4. It is the mental building block of your team. If you can learn to believe and motivate yourself to find four, and they can do the same, then your mindset fuels the growth.

# The Product Sales

Compared to the rest of the cornerstones, people are the most important and most challenging aspect to understand, believe in, and motivate. Product sales, however, are not.

In a legitimate Network Marketing business, the distributors are very satisfied customers … with unbridled enthusiasm. They love the product. **They love it so much that they start recommending it.**

The average Network Marketer might only personally use and sell $100–$300 worth of product a month. There will always be exceptions. There are people who sell thousands a month. But as long as the product is compelling, the distributors will sell it … or more accurately, recommend it.

Some will ask after seeing all the geometric progressions of recruiting, "Well, if everyone is recruiting, who will sell the product?" I like to let people think for a moment about what they just asked. The answer is akin to "Who is buried in Grant's Tomb?" Everyone is selling the product. And the more people we have selling it, the more we sell. We just don't worry about how much any one distributor sells.

Sales are simply created by the distributors using and offering products. So if you have 340 distributors each averaging $200 a month in consumption and sales, your business would generate $68,000 a month in sales. **Try personally selling $68,000 a month of any product.** You would have to work about 1,000 hours a week. Your family would not like it.

**At Bliss Business we teach a very natural and simple way of recommending your product.** *Just listen.* Listen to the people around you. Listen to what they talk about. When you hear them talk about a problem that your product solved for you, just ask them if you can tell them your story. Tell your story and ask them if they would be willing to *"just take a look."*

You do not need 100 customers to build a successful Four Year Career. If everyone had 5–10 customers, the personal sales volume would be $1,000–$2,000, not the $200 described here.

# The Asset Income

This is the easiest cornerstone to understand and believe. Every Network Marketing company has a compensation plan that pays you on most, if not all, of the many generations of distributors in your group. **This is the percent of sales volume you will earn on each generation of leaders.**

Every company is very creative to incentivize (yes, this is now a word) certain business-building behaviors. The bottom line is that you can expect to earn between 5% and 10% on the sales of most of your organization, and even a small percent on all of it, providing you qualify to earn at the deepest generations. This gives you Asset Income.

## IF YOUR TEAM'S SALES ARE $68,000 A MONTH, YOU ARE EARNING BETWEEN $3,400 – $7,000.

We use an average of 7% in most of our modeling. A younger sales team (as in how many years the team has been in place) will lean toward 10% and an older one will trend toward 5%.

**EARNED INCOME**

- Always paid LESS than you are worth
- Your employer needs to profit on your time
- You don't show up for a day, you don't get paid
- You don't show up for 3 days, and you don't ever get paid again
- The income is worth the income ... period
- You can only increase marginally ... no quantum increases

**ASSET INCOME (AFTER IT IS RESIDUAL)**

- Earn what you are worth as a Creator of Revenue
- Build it and earn on it, potentially forever
- Take time off and get paid anyway
- Semi-retire on full pay
- The asset is worth 200 times the monthly income
- Law of 200 ... income grows, potentially geometrically

EARNED INCOME IS GREAT FOR PAYING THE BILLS.
ASSET INCOME PAYS FOR LIFE.

# The Asset Value

If you continue to use the theoretical model of four who enroll four, etc., then at some point, perhaps around year two or three, 256 people would fill your fourth generation of leaders.

This would result in a total of 340 people in your Network Marketing organization. **If each of those leaders uses and recommends just $200 of product per month, there would be 340 people selling a total of $68,000 worth of product monthly.**

If you were paid an average royalty of 7% on that $68,000, your monthly check would be $4,760.

If you could count on it continuing long after you were done building it, then it would be deemed residual and would have a corresponding asset value. **$6,800 a month, for example, is worth about $1,200,000 using The Law of 200.**

> **Note: All examples in this book are hypotheticals. Remember: only 5% of Network Marketers attempt to build an Asset Income and less than 1% build anything of substance. The only income possibilities you should rely on are those contained in a particular company's "Income Disclosure Statement." If a copy of it is not included with this book, ask for it. It will give you the annual income averages at all levels.**

# WHAT IS THE LAW OF 200?

Your residual income is worth 200 times the monthly income.

Examples of other income-producing assets would be real estate, dividend-producing stocks, and patent and copyright royalties. All of these can be appraised for a value based on their income histories and future income prospects.

*So how do you know it will be residual?*

## The Answer . . . Is in the Numbers

Look closely at the generations diagram that follows. Which generation earns you the most income?

Let's look at your first generation. In the diagram, there are four leaders shown. If they are each producing $200 in sales, then in total they are producing $800. Your second generation is producing $3,200. Your third is producing $12,800. Your fourth $51,200.

Obviously, it is the fourth generation, which has four times as many people in it as the third generation before it. **In fact, more than 75% of your group's sales volume—and therefore, over 75% of your earnings—are from your fourth-generation sales leaders.**

In this scenario, however, we are showing your fourth-generation leaders as just getting started in the business. As sales leaders *"doing it,"* they are inviting others to have a look, but they have not yet enrolled anyone themselves according to the diagram, as we *do not show a fifth generation.*

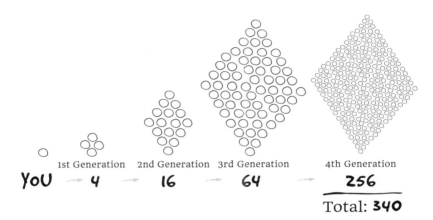

| | 1st Generation | 2nd Generation | 3rd Generation | 4th Generation |
|---|---|---|---|---|
| YoU | 4 | 16 | 64 | 256 |

Total: **340**

Note: **All examples in this book are hypotheticals. Remember: only 5% of Network Marketers attempt to build an Asset Income and less than 1% build anything of substance. The only income possibilities you should rely on are those contained in a particular company's "Income Disclosure Statement." If a copy of it is not included with this book, ask for it. It will give you the annual income averages at all levels.**

When each fourth-generation sales leader gets their four, you would have added 1,024 new distributors to your fifth generation. **At $200 per distributor in sales that translates into an additional $204,800 in sales.**

# THIS ONE PIECE OF THE PUZZLE PULLS IT ALL TOGETHER. WHEN YOU UNDERSTAND THIS PIECE, YOU ARE LIKELY TO "GET IT" AND START TO UNDERSTAND THE POSSIBILITIES OF THE FOUR YEAR CAREER.

Everyone we have shown thus far in this hypothetical plan is a sales leader. We have shown that each one gets four.

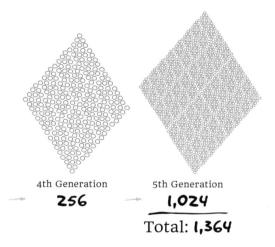

4th Generation
**256**

5th Generation
**1,024**

Total: **1,364**

In order to get four to actually *"do this"* and be a sales leader, each will have to enroll many more than just four. Your first four are not likely going to be *"the four."* **Each sales leader will likely enroll 20–100 people in order to get their own four sales leaders.** The point is, in The Four Year Career, we only show sales leaders. They are not the best of the best, just the best of the rest. They didn't quit. They are doing it.

What about all the non-sales leaders? What about the majority of new distributors who did not end up "doing it"? Some quit and never continue even using the product. Some give up on the income option but remain loyal customers. Some sell a little, and some even enroll a few people here and there. But they are not sales leaders and NONE of them are shown in this plan. **So what if you add them back in?**

FOUR YEARS FROM NOW, IF YOU BUILD YOUR FOUR YEAR CAREER, YOU WILL HAVE MORE SALES FROM CUSTOMERS AND DISTRIBUTORS AS A TOTAL GROUP THAN FROM SALES LEADERS ... FAR MORE.

|  | 1st<br>Generation | 2nd<br>Generation | 3rd<br>Generation | 4th<br>Generation |
|---|---|---|---|---|
| You → | 4 → | 16 → | 64 → | 256 |

Total: **340**

## $200 sales each x 340 people = $68,000

If each person has $200 in sales, that's 340 people earning total sales of $68,000. You could earn an average of 7%* on all of it per month:

## $68,000 x 7%* = $4,760 a month = $1,000,000 Asset Value

$4,760 a month for example is worth about $1,000,000 at a 10% annualized return over the course of 10 years.

*Industry average

> Note: All examples in this book are hypotheticals. Remember: only 5% of Network Marketers attempt to build an Asset Income and less than 1% build anything of substance. The only income possibilities you should rely on are those contained in a particular company's "Income Disclosure Statement." If a copy of it is not included with this book, ask for it. It will give you the annual income averages at all levels.

Network Marketing can actually give you the access and the key to the vault in the other net worth-building investment models.

### NOW YOUR "EXTRA FEW THOUSAND A MONTH" IS WORTH A GREAT DEAL MORE.

# THE POWER OF PACE

"THE SECRET TO MAKING THE COMPOUNDING EFFECT WORK FOR YOU ... IS THAT FIRST YOU HAVE TO BREAK THROUGH INERTIA."

— Richard Bliss Brooke

L aunching a Network Marketing sales group is much like pushing a car over a very slight hill. Imagine that you ran out of gas as you were driving up a hill. At the top of the hill the road becomes flat for some period of time and then slightly descends to the bottom of the hill where there is a gas station. **Your mission is to get out of the car, get it rolling up the slight hill, to the top, and keep it going on the flat section until you crest the hill.** Then you hop in and go for the ride of your life.

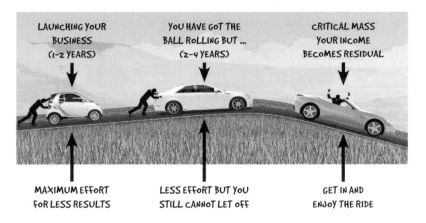

Another example is getting a plane to take off. It requires FULL POWER until rotation speed or liftoff. You cannot start and stop or give it half power. You will never get it off the ground.

Network Marketing is the same. In the beginning, you will exert the most amount of effort promoting the product and enrolling new people for the least amount of return. Once you get things rolling, it will take less effort, but you must still keep pushing to keep it going.

**Once you gain momentum, you just hop in and enjoy the ride.**

Momentum happens at different times in different companies. You will know it when you are in it. You will not be able to keep up with the requests people have for you, and your group will be on fire.

It is the low return on effort in the beginning that leads most people to give up. **They do not have the vision and belief in the payoffs on the other side.**

Yet if you understand the power of Geometric Progression and compounding, then you KNOW if you keep **doubling a penny a day, it is worth over $5 million at the end of the month.**

## PACE: KEEP DOUBLING

| DAY 15 | DAY 21 | DAY 26 | DAY 30 |
|--------|--------|--------|--------|
| $163 | $10,500 | $335,000 | $5 Million |

**AFTER 30 DAYS, ONE PENNY BECOMES OVER $5 MILLION!**

> Note: All examples in this book are hypotheticals. Remember: only 5% of Network Marketers attempt to build an Asset Income and less than 1% build anything of substance. The only income possibilities you should rely on are those contained in a particular company's "Income Disclosure Statement." If a copy of it is not included with this book, ask for it. It will give you the annual income averages at all levels.

Now let's look at the results if we slow our pace of play …

If it took a lot of effort to double that penny, given the return on investment of effort, most people would quit. Even halfway through the month, it is **only worth $163.84!**

## SLOWER PACE: DOUBLING EVERY OTHER DAY

| Day 1 | $0.01 | Day 17 | $2.56 |
|-------|-------|--------|-------|
| Day 3 | $0.02 | Day 19 | $5.12 |
| Day 5 | $0.04 | Day 21 | $10.24 |
| Day 7 | $0.08 | Day 23 | $20.48 |
| Day 9 | $0.16 | Day 25 | $40.96 |
| Day 11 | $0.32 | Day 27 | $81.92 |
| Day 13 | $0.64 | Day 29 | $163.84 |
| Day 15 | $1.28 | | |

AFTER 29 DAYS, ONE PENNY BECOMES ONLY $163.81!

Pace of play matters. **Which would you rather have?**

# THE MOTIVATION TRAP

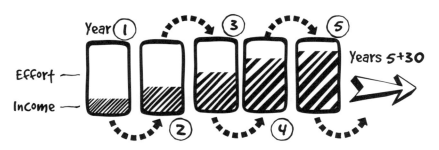

THE MOTIVATION TRAP OF NETWORK MARKETING IS YOU GET PAID THE LEAST DURING THE YEARS YOUR EFFORTS ARE THE HIGHEST. MOST PEOPLE DO NOT HAVE THE VISION AND SELF-MOTIVATION TO WORK THE MOST DURING A PERIOD OF TIME WHEN THEY GET PAID THE LEAST.

WHAT THEY FAIL TO SEE AND BELIEVE IS THAT IF THEY DO THE WORK, THEY CAN GET PAID THE HIGHEST INCOME FOR THE LEAST AMOUNT OF EFFORT IN LATER YEARS, AND THOSE YEARS CAN LAST A LIFETIME, AS OPPOSED TO THE TRAP YEARS, WHICH MAY ONLY BE THE FIRST AND SECOND YEARS.

THOSE WHO SUCCEED LEARN TO UNDERSTAND THAT THE WORK IS WORTH IT.

# THE POWER of PERSONAL DEVELOPMENT

"IF YOU ARE GOING TO INVEST, DO SO IN SOMETHING YOU ALREADY OWN, WITH THE GREATEST POTENTIAL FOR A 10-FOLD RETURN ... YOU."

— Richard Bliss Brooke

Yes, it is true that building a sales organization of on-fire volunteers is a challenge. However, it is being done, and in a powerful way. **The biggest challenge is in erasing people's negative beliefs and biases** about the Network Marketing concept and replacing them with what those of us who have already done it know to be true. And, it's coming. One day soon, world consciousness will shift and many people—perhaps most people—will in some way be a part of this dynamic wealth-building industry.

Opportunity appreciation is not the only factor fueling the future of Network Marketing. It is also fueled by people's basic needs to connect with others, to be a part of something bigger than themselves, and to **have a sense of community**.

Most of us know all too well that the family model has disintegrated in many segments of our country. Since **family is the foundation of neighborhoods and communities**, they too have been compromised. Most of the industrialized world is deeply entrenched in the rat race—parents with full-time careers, day care, career advancement, soccer, music lessons, email, social media, cell phones, payments, payments, and more payments.

## SOME OF US ARE WINNING THE RAT RACE, BUT AS IT'S BEEN SAID, "WE ARE STILL RATS!"

Today, people are longing for a return to a real, safe, relaxed time of freedom and soulful connection with others. **People want to play together, pray together, get to really know each other, and most importantly, be known by others.**

We want to improve ourselves, to have more pride in ourselves, and to love and respect ourselves. We are hungry for guidance and support that will help us grow to be more powerful, more generous, and more self-assured. Anyone who has come full circle can tell you that these are the things that bring true happiness.

Achieving financial success and status is wonderful, especially if the alternative is being financially strapped to a life of despair. I think we'd all be better off rich, but **money is relative—the more you have, the more you think you need.**

Or, as it's been said:

## "MONEY IS RELATIVE. THE MORE MONEY YOU HAVE, THE MORE RELATIVES YOU HAVE."

This return to **basic human values** in business is a subtle, yet powerful, force driving the Network Marketing industry.

These are the qualities that will endear you to your family and to the community you create:

| | | |
|---|---|---|
| Patience | Honesty | Forthrightness |
| Generosity | Integrity | Leadership |
| Open-mindedness | Authenticity | Love |
| Cooperation | Courage | Listening |

Network Marketing may offer the most dynamic environment for us to develop our spirituality, while managing our humanity at the same time. It may just be the most exciting leadership and character development program you have ever imagined. *Are you up for that?*

# WHAT TO LOOK FOR IN A NETWORK MARKETING COMPANY

"LEND YOUR EFFORTS AND REPUTATION TO A COMPANY THAT HONORS YOUR VALUES AND PHILOSOPHIES."

— Richard Bliss Brooke

**C**hoosing your company wisely is the single most important thing you can do for your future in Network Marketing.

It's kind of like choosing someone to marry.

**Ladies**, did you or would you marry the first guy who drove up in a sports car and offered to buy you one too?

**Guys**, did you or would you marry the first lady who let you touch her body?

We meet, watch, and listen to a lot of people before we get married. And if you've made a mistake in marriage, well, you know all too well how important it is to your net worth, income, health, and peace of mind to make a solid, values-based choice next time.

# Here Is What to Look For:

## 1. Products You Love

The most important ingredient in your success is the products you choose to recommend. The products create the income. No commissions are ever paid on enrollments, team building, or events. Your income is tied directly to product sales, and your **Asset Income is tied to REPEAT product sales ... customers who use and buy every month for LIFE**.

Anything less than this and you are building a house of cards. And you are building, at best, Earned Income vs. Asset Income.

Ask yourself this question: If you do build a team, whether it's a team of 20, 200, or 2,000, how long do you want to get paid on what you built? Is 10 years enough? 20 years? 30 years? Yes, maybe it sounds like it now, but it won't sound like it six months before the end of your term. Face it. If you build it, you want to, and should, get paid forever ... including generations of your family after you.

━━━━━━━━━━━━━━

**IN SOME COMPANIES, THERE ARE ALREADY THREE GENERATIONS OF FAMILY THAT GET PAID FROM WHAT THE GREAT-GRANDPARENTS BUILT. WHY NOT YOU?**

━━━━━━━━━━━━━━

The most important aspect of a product is:

**YOU ABSOLUTELY LOVE THE PRODUCT AND WILL USE IT INSTEAD OF ANY COMPETITIVE PRODUCT, FOREVER, REGARDLESS OF WHETHER YOU EVER SELL IT. YOU WILL ALWAYS BE "A CUSTOMER."**

It does not matter that there are similar products, even less expensive products, in the marketplace. A BMW is similar to a Mercedes, as is a Lexus. They all prosper based on customers that will only own their particular brand. These customers love the features, benefits, look, feel, performance, and THE BRAND, and cannot ever foresee changing.

## 2. Retention Rate

___

"NOTHING WORTHWHILE REALLY EVER COMES EASILY. WORK, CONTINUOUS WORK AND HARD WORK, IS THE ONLY WAY YOU WILL ACCOMPLISH RESULTS THAT LAST. WHATEVER YOU WANT IN LIFE, YOU MUST GIVE UP SOMETHING TO GET IT. THE GREATER THE VALUE, THE GREATER THE SACRIFICE REQUIRED OF YOU.

THERE'S A PRICE TO PAY IF YOU WANT TO MAKE THINGS BETTER, A PRICE TO PAY FOR JUST LEAVING THINGS AS THEY ARE. THE HIGHWAY TO SUCCESS IS A TOLL ROAD. EVERYTHING HAS A PRICE."

— Unknown

___

Retention is the second most important aspect to your success. Retention refers to how many people join your team or become customers and stay on as customers or team members.

For example, if you enroll 10 customers, and a year from now only 2 are still customers, your customer retention rate is 20%. If you enroll 20 people to build a business with you, and a year from now you have 1 still building your sales force, your retention rate is 5%.

**Retention rate is the Holy Grail of wealth building, the secret metric for success in Network Marketing.** Low retention or *"leaky bucket"* syndrome means that you'll have to be constantly replacing those who quit. Customer retention is obviously huge, as it speaks directly to the value of your product. Value is created by the actual performance of the product in the hands of your customers in relation to the price charged. A product may produce good results, but if the price is high in relation to the results, retention will be lower.

---

## YOU WANT TO BE PROMOTING A PRODUCT THAT HAS VERY HIGH VALUE ... A POWERFUL CUSTOMER EXPERIENCE FOR A PRICE THEY ARE WILLING TO PAY.

---

Salesforce retention speaks to recruiting. Finding your 4 sales leaders at a 5% retention rate requires a lot of recruiting, up to 80 people to find your 4. However, if your retention rate is 20%, you may only have to recruit 20.

The less recruiting that is required, the more time everyone can spend promoting the actual products, and the quicker those working toward their Four Year Careers can enjoy it.

Historically, one of the real downfalls of the Network Marketing model has been that, oftentimes, the products marketed do not have attractive long-term value. Claims about performance may be very high, therefore the price is high ... *but the results are not experienced.*

# ON THE RANCH, WE CALL THAT "ALL HAT AND NO CATTLE."

One of the most powerful questions you can ask before joining a company is *what is the retention rate ... both for customers and sales leaders?*

It should be a number tracked company-wide and internally by each sales leader. Ask for it. **If you cannot get it, beware.**

Look for a retention rate of at least 20% for customers and 10% for sales leaders. Some companies are achieving up to 50%. The impact on your Four Year Career can be astounding.

For example, compare a **retention rate of 10% vs. 50%**. Retention is related to compounding. You need to compound a lot faster to make up for low retention.

As an analogy, imagine that you have 100 people on your team. Let's say 100 team members is like having $100,000 cash invested. Compare a compounded growth rate of 10% vs. 50%. (This is a related analogy, not a direct one.)

# RETENTION COMPOUNDED

## 10%

In 7 years you will have:

**$194,871.71**

vs.

## 50%

In 7 years you will have:

**$1,708,593.75**

In 14 years you will have:

**$379,749.03**

vs.

In 14 years you will have:

**$29,192,926.63**

Note: All examples in this book are hypotheticals. Remember: only 5% of Network Marketers attempt to build an Asset Income and less than 1% build anything of substance. The only income possibilities you should rely on are those contained in a particular company's "Income Disclosure Statement." If a copy of it is not included with this book, ask for it. It will give you the annual income averages at all levels.

Pick your product wisely. Ask the right questions. If you're going to invest 4–10 years of your life building your future, **do it with an extraordinary product**.

## 3. Hype vs. Track Record

Which is more important to you: The possibility of earning $20,000 a month for a few months or years and then looking for a new and better opportunity? Or, earning $5,000 a month, every month, for the next 50 years?

**How do you know a company will be here for the next 50 years?** Based on what they tell you? Do you listen to promises or do you look at what they have already done?

Promises are nothing more than hype. **Hype is marketing spin:** promotions, claims, and lots and lots of shiny objects. Fish like them. We know these promises are probably not all true ... not exactly, or maybe not at all ... but we like hearing them. They help us believe, and we so want to believe.

When you hear things like:

- We are the fastest growing company
- We have made more millionaires than any other company
- We are the next billion-dollar company
- We have reinvented Network Marketing
- Timing is everything, and THIS is the right time
- If you don't join today, you will MISS the opportunity

- our products are better than any other product
- All the top networkers are joining
- This product sells itself

Or any other BS like this, run for the exits ... unless you like starting over again and again and again.

If you want to get paid for 50 years, doesn't it make sense to first look at the companies that have proven they can and will pay you for 50 years?

And if you don't find the product or culture you're looking for, check out the 25-year-old companies ...

Then the 15-year-old ones ...
Then the 10 ...
Then the 7.

The younger the company, the more risk you incur, as their track record is shorter. Startups are the riskiest, yet every billion-dollar company was once a startup.

## 4. Burning Man or an Honorable Culture?

Culture is defined by a set of common values that are held up high and important to the group, values that anchor every new product, every event, every program, and every word written and spoken by the leaders of the group. Someone who does not subscribe to the culture can exist inside of it, but not comfortably and not successfully.

**What is more important to you?** Operating in an environment where anything goes … you can do your own thing and create your own culture (or none at all). Or, operating in an environment that has expectations based on a common set of values.

Here's what I look for in a culture … an extreme culture that matches my values: honesty, integrity, vulnerability, fun, leadership, personal development, and honor. When I say "extreme," I mean that the **culture screams at the world who they are**. I want that from the owner on down … everyone is held accountable to express the culture.

I want these rules. I want this order. It helps me become a better man. Let me loose for the rest of my life at Burning Man and I will explode in a burst of indiscretions. And I expect most people would. I want to be around people I can trust to protect me and my honor, to hold me accountable to do right.

And I want culture because it is essential for longevity of the organization. A culture that matches my values will fend off the cancer of greed and competition. All great societies are rich in culture. Everything else is just a frat party.

## CHOOSE WISELY, MY FRIEND.

# YOU CREATE YOUR OWN ODDS

"YOU CAN DEFY THE ODDS BY CREATING THE ODDS.
ONLY YOU DECIDE IF YOU ARE TO BE THE ONE."

— Richard Bliss Brooke

# The Probability Quiz

Here are 12 statements. Check each one that is **TRUE** for you. Obviously, the more boxes you check, the better candidate you are to succeed in your own Four Year Career.

☐ I DO have some things YET to do in my life ... things that may be a stretch for me.

☐ I DO have some things YET I want to have ... that also may be a stretch for me.

☐ I DO have some things YET I want to be ... smarter, stronger, kinder, and more generous.

☐ I CAN choose, on most days, to be happy, positive, and grateful.

☐ I KNOW in my heart that I am responsible for where I am in my life and do not blame others.

☐ I ENJOY other people and find I am naturally curious about their lives.

☐ I LISTEN more than I talk ... or at least I would love to learn how to.

☐ I generally KEEP my word. If I tell someone I am going to do something or be somewhere, they can count on me.

☐ I FIND the time to do what needs to be done to achieve my goals.

☐ My integrity, reputation, and relationships are more important to me than more income.

☐ I WANT more out of my life ... relationships, love, fun, adventure, challenges, and learning.

☐ I BELIEVE in myself ... not all the time, but often enough. I would love to BELIEVE in myself all the time.

Total up your check marks: _____

Let the person who gave you this book know what score you have.

A lot of what I have shared in this book is opinion; some of it is factual.

The one thing I intended to present here is that **Network Marketing as a wealth-building model *works*.** That is indisputable. It is factual. Network Marketing is legal, and it is even honorable.

Does it work often enough for most people? No, it does not.

Franchising, on the other hand, or a master's degree in a chosen profession, does work most of the time for most people.

**The difference is what you invest in time and resources.**

A franchise will cost you perhaps everything you have with zero recourse if it does not work. No one is giving you your money back on unsold merchandise. Nor is anyone guaranteeing you a rewarding career in exchange for your master's degree ... and they are certainly not going to forgive your student debt.

I celebrate both of those investments for those who are inspired to pursue them.

I also celebrate this model ... a model that requires a very small investment. A model you can pursue whenever and wherever you choose. A model that may not pay well in the beginning but can pay handsomely for a lifetime. A model that does not discriminate based on age, religion, nationality, handicap, wealth, or education ... but rather, **a model that rewards ambition, being coachable, attitude, energy, passion, and a profound curiosity for other people.**

And I know this: just because most people do not succeed is no reason to discourage YOU if you want to succeed. Imagine your child wanting to be a professional dancer or actor or athlete. What would your attitude and coaching be? *Forget about it. Your odds of success are 1 in 100,000.* Or, would you encourage them to be one of the one?

The odds of success in Network Marketing for YOU are not 1 in 100,000 or 1 in 10,000 or even 1 in 1,000. **Your odds are your odds.** They are based on the product you choose to promote, the company that offers the product, and YOU.

Having worked with thousands of people since 1977, I can tell you this for sure: **anyone can make this work for them**. All skills and attitudes are learned. All beliefs are learned. You cannot teach a fish to climb a tree, but you can teach a human being to find a product they love, share their story, and invite others to *"just take a look"* at the income option.

I learned how to go from a negative, cynical, introverted chicken chopper to something much more. And it was the culture and community of Network Marketing that fostered that growth.

WHETHER YOUR ACTUAL ODDS ARE 1 IN 100 OR 1 IN 1,000, YOU CAN BE YOUR ONE OF THE ONE.

# What Is Your Next Step?

You can do nothing, and I appreciate you reading this book.

You can pass it on to someone you feel might respond to it.

You can contact the person who gave the book to you, if it was a gift, and ask them to tell you about their product.

Or if you have already found your passion, you can study *The Four Year Career®*...

---

**LEARN TO BELIEVE IN IT, TEACH IT, AND BUILD ONE FOR YOURSELF.**

---

# SUCCESS STORIES

The following stories feature people who may be much like you. Certainly in the beginning, they didn't understand or necessarily believe in the possibilities of Network Marketing. And as you will read, most were not instant successes. Many of them have the same stories as most people during their first few months or even years … "This doesn't work!"

Yet, if you can reflect on the examples of duplication, compounding, and the car over the hill, it might help you make sense of these massive success stories. This is a much bigger opportunity than most people believe. And that is the promise of Network Marketing … that it is just an opportunity. What you do with it is up to you.

These stories are a sample of people I know who have made it big in Network Marketing and did it in an ethical and responsible manner in a company of the same character.

## DISCLAIMER

These success stories are exceptional exceptions and are shared here to inspire you and show you people from different walks of life who have succeeded. They are not what you should expect to accomplish. They are 1 out of 10,000 or less. And yet it is interesting to note where they came from and what they accomplished. And maybe, just maybe, you could do the same.

# LAURA EVANS

Isle of Palms, South Carolina

## NEVER MISS A MOMENT

As a successful corporate executive, Laura missed watching her 4 kids grow up. Now she's moved out of her company's executive offices to become an independent Network Marketing business owner with a thriving international team and time freedom.

For 25 years, Laura had a successful career as a Sales & Marketing Executive, working for companies such as J.Crew, Disney, and even a few well-known Network Marketing companies. Yet her success came at a price.

Even though she was financially and professionally successful, this wife and mother of four children felt conflicted between work and family. Sacrificing quality time with her loved ones, as she strived to provide for them, became the norm. Work consumed Laura's life, and her family had what little, if any, was left over.

Laura was first introduced to the business opportunity by a colleague who invited her to an event. The business looked interesting, but she couldn't see herself walking away from a six-figure career level income, and didn't quite have the courage to try.

After experiencing a transformational shape change and weight loss on the products, Laura's friends and family began asking, "What are you doing?" It was at that moment that she realized, "I CAN have my own business; I CAN do this!"

Within Laura's first year of leaving Corporate America, she personally recruited 105 team members. By the second year, her team was 6,550 strong. Her third year, she had a team of 8,725. Four years in, Laura's team now numbers 87,133 and is producing over $540,000 a month in sales.

Laura quickly learned that success comes not from selling but from listening. As her business grew and she replaced her full-time income with Network Marketing, her focus shifted from being a six-figure earner to a six-figure GIVER. She developed a culture of caring and celebration. One of her favorite quotes is from Theodore Roosevelt: "People do not care how much you know, until they know how much you care."

For Laura, life now includes all the things she used to miss out on, such as first days of school, field trips, graduations, birthdays, and holidays. Another perk is living where she and her husband want to live, which is on an island in Charleston, SC.

*This success story is not typical and is shared to inspire you and show you what's possible. It is not what you should expect to accomplish.*

# DOUG & CHARLENE FIKE

Washington, DC

## GLOBAL IMPACT FUNDED BY PART-TIME BUSINESS

The Fikes started their business in college to fund their global leadership commitments, empowering communities from Survival to Significance. They "world-schooled" their kids, and after a 16-year hiatus, returned as active Network Marketers at the company's highest rank.

When Doug was growing up, the Network Marketing products were always a part of his home. He'd witnessed transformations, both in his family's health and in the ecology of the mountain community where his parents were missionaries. His parents' business helped them build a new life and put their kids through college after returning from the mission field.

Doug understood the power of the products ... but it took Charlene, whom he met in college, to recognize that the business could be their own God-given avenue to freedom. They started building their Network Marketing business as full-time college students while leading a thriving campus ministry.

Charlene was finishing a social work degree, but was struggling with the thought of a lifetime spent working within entrenched bureaucracies. She was looking for the means to make a real difference and the freedom to do life on her own terms. Creating a business with the company Doug grew up in was a perfect fit, creating possibilities beyond anything the young dreamers could have conceived.

"Our business is not the most important thing in our lives," they have always said. "It allows us to do the things that are!" Always working part time, they built a thriving business while starting churches and resourcing a growing leadership network. Their strong family focus allowed them to "world-school" their kids, and in time, launch a range of creative initiatives with their adult children.

Following their first decade, Doug and Charlene took a 16-year hiatus from the business, which enabled them to purchase a country estate in Virginia's Allegheny Highlands, running a country inn and creating a place of retreat for weary global-change agents. Charlene also pursued her passion to empower marginalized women in developing nations, while Doug resourced leaders and pursued peacemaking initiatives in global conflict zones.

A fateful conversation with their twenty-something son relaunched a new business era. "Mom & Dad, you owe it to my generation to help us discover how to live the kind of lives you've been able to live!" he'd exclaimed. Charlene took the challenge, coming out of retirement to enable a new generation to embrace the 21st century opportunity—pursuing their own dreams and "Crafting Lives That Matter!"

# LAURA HOSTETLER

Camden, Ohio & Key Largo, Florida

## CHALLENGES THAT DON'T DEFEAT YOU JUST MAKE YOU STRONGER

Laura grew up in Network Marketing but wasn't handed anything. Despite severe family issues, financial struggles, health challenges, and the loss of two children, she has emerged as a leader of one of her company's most powerful organizations.

Laura started life as so many people do. She worked too hard, worked far too long, and never reaped any of the benefits of her arduous labor. After years of hard work on the family dairy farm, Laura married young and set out to see the world for all its glory.

Unfortunately, plans never quite work out exactly the way they are set. Laura's were derailed by the tragic and sudden death of her first child, and that wasn't the end of her hardships.

The family dairy business collapsed as the economy changed, and then a tornado wiped out the rest of their life's work. Left with a mountain of debt from uninsured liabilities, life's possibilities were looking a little bleak. The family's financial woes only compounded when her husband was struck by illness and given only a six-month prognosis.

That's when Laura knew she had to become the family income earner.

Even though the dairy farm business was wiped out, what remained was the Network Marketing business her parents had started. Laura put her nose to the grindstone, redirecting her strong work ethic into building her own success in their existing Network Marketing business.

She worked to define her own role and went on to triple her family's income in just 9 months and earn the top-ranking position within the company. Sure, she faced hurdle after hurdle on her journey to financial freedom, yet she was fueled by unwavering conviction, deep faith, and a passion to pour herself into helping others.

The youngest of seven children, Laura always knew it would take a plan, hard work, and determination to reach her goal. Since joining the Network Marketing business that her parents began, she's sponsored several hundred people, many of whom are living lives of financial freedom.

When a person connects inner values with a goal, anything is possible. Dreams can be achieved, and goals can be met. For Laura, financial freedom means the ability to work in a field she loves, travel when and where she wants, and to know that she has earned every ounce of her success. Building a generational business has given her security … something no one can ever take away. The accomplishment of not compromising who she was along the way, regardless of the challenges, was her greatest success.

# BARB & RAY MADORIN

Scottsdale, Arizona

## BUILD YOUR DREAMS BY BUILDING OTHER PEOPLE'S DREAMS

Barb started her business with powerful family product results and encouragement from her global executive husband. Ray understood the potential for building an income-producing asset. Now working as a team, they are role models and international Network Marketing mentors and coaches.

Barb worked briefly in banking before she and her husband, Ray, decided she'd stay at home until their boys were in school. The boys were just 1 and 3 years old when Barb heard a radio interview about an environmentally safe cleaning product. Then a friend from church invited her to an event featuring that company.

Although Barb was fascinated by the products, the thought of membership and what it might require scared her, so she became a customer instead. A year later, after 6 invitations to attend another meeting, she finally decided to join. Barb realized she could make money from home, qualify for the car they desperately needed, and maybe even afford a family trip, just by offering healthy products to others.

After a physical issue Barb had dealt with for years unexpectedly disappeared within weeks of using the nutritional products, she was all in. Her first year, she earned more than $18,000—a lot of money at that time. She was expanding with others locally and across the country, and focused her attention on personal development. Those who were growing were getting stronger emotionally, spiritually and intellectually.

The rewards to their family have been considerable. They qualified for one particularly memorable trip to France, Italy and Monte Carlo when the boys were 10 and 12. Barb says, "They have been able to do things and go places that most people will never be able to do. More importantly, I can offer this gift to others."

Six years ago, Ray joined her in the business. It's something they'd talked about for years; it just took him a while, coming from a corporate background, to figure out that he wanted to take this profession on. While their boys were growing up, Ray had traveled the globe in his high-level business position and did very well. His regret was that he was not around most of the time.

They've had adjustments to make, but have found they make a really good team. Their organization now produces $2-3 million a year in sales all over North America. It's been fun for them to see the growth in each other and the resulting growth in their organization.

They say, "It takes working to support others in building their dreams in order for us to achieve ours. We love teaching leadership and profitability. The satisfaction in seeing others succeed is indescribable. And giving back with our time, energy and finances to people and causes we believe in is such a bonus."

# ROLAND OOSTERHOUSE

Nashville, Tennessee

## BE COURAGEOUS AND CHANGE YOUR LIFE

Though haunted by a teacher telling him "you'll never succeed," Roland gathered the courage to leave his hometown, go to college, and eventually say yes to Network Marketing. Today this 40+ year leader is a powerful global inspiration.

Born and raised in Michigan, Roland spent the first 18 years of his life living and working on his family's farm. He was very proud that these experiences gave him the opportunity to develop some entrepreneurial skills.

However, Roland's entrepreneurial spirit was crushed when a school counselor told him: "You're a bump on a log and will never amount to anything." Roland was also told that he wouldn't be able to hold a job and that he would never be able to make it through college.

Those words haunted him every day.

After high school, Roland got a job in a factory, thinking that this type of work would be what he would be doing for the rest of his life. One day at the factory, a fellow worker said, "Why don't you go to California and go to college?" Roland was too terrified to tell him of the words that were haunting him. Fortunately, he summoned the courage to start a new life.

While in California, he took a few college courses to see if he could possibly get a passing grade. Much to his surprise, he was successful and was encouraged to continue his education. Roland graduated from San Fernando Valley State University with a BA degree in communications.

A few years prior, while working in a service station, someone introduced him to a product that was sold by a Network Marketing company. Even though Roland enjoyed the product and told other people about it, he was very hesitant to look at the business plan for fear he would not be successful, especially being an introvert.

After seeing people enjoying the product, Roland started looking at his company's magazine and saw others who were successful in the business. This inspired him to say yes to the opportunity.

Six months later, the multiplication factor really started to work. After two and a half years, his income was enough at that time to support his growing family. He reached the top rank in his company in the first few years. Roland has now been in Network Marketing for over 47 years with the same company and has distributors in seven countries.

He says, "It's the friends you make, the self-development, and helping others that makes Network Marketing so rewarding. Another great benefit is that your children will learn invaluable entrepreneurial skills. It's all about making a positive difference for yourself and others."

---

*This success story is not typical and is shared to inspire you and show you what's possible. It is not what you should expect to accomplish.*

# CHRIS & JESSICA PAGE

Watertown, New York

## FROM LOCAL TO GLOBAL IMPACT

When Chris and Jessica began making more from Network Marketing than from their 7-figure fitness training business, they had their big A-ha moment. They jumped in feet first and are now helping fitness trainers across the globe create their dream lifestyles.

Chris and Jessica were very successful fitness business entrepreneurs. Together they owned and operated a large personal training business with a staff of 20. However, their huge facility was also accompanied by a huge overhead of more than $50,000 a month.

Although successful, both realized the benefit that an additional revenue stream could offer their business. So when a longtime family friend of Jessica's introduced them to nutritional supplements from a Network Marketing company, the timing couldn't have been better.

Jessica says, "Nutritional supplements made the most sense for our fitness business. We were missing this important key element in our client programs. Ultimately, this impacted their success as well as our own."

Chris has a degree in Human Physiology and was skeptical of the products. "You don't see causation studies with nutritional supplements, so when I see compelling science my radar goes off and my guard goes up. But I quickly realized I had been introduced to a company whose products were exactly what they said they were, their values resonated with my own, and I knew I could passionately recommend them to our clients," Chris recalls.

They began customizing nutritional supplement plans for each training client but soon recognized the need to systematize the process. Chris says, "We had systems in place for all other areas of our business. Network Marketing is a business and should be treated as one, so we made sure to give it the high priority it deserved."

Soon after, they noticed exponential growth in that area of their business. It didn't take long before they were earning more net profit from the Network Marketing products than they were from their 7-figure training business.

"We saw how other fitness businesses were struggling and frustrated with low earnings. We were getting hit up all the time on what we were doing. That's when we had our A-ha moment," they say.

Chris and Jessica knew they could provide other fitness business owners the same freedoms through Network Marketing and implementing those same systems into their businesses.

That's when they both jumped in feet first and started building their four-year career. Two years later they had built a network of hundreds of fitness businesses and personal trainers, from all over North America, who were creating their own dream lifestyles and better serving their clients.

*This success story is not typical and is shared to inspire you and show you what's possible. It is not what you should expect to accomplish.*

# GENE & NEDRA SAHR

Eliot, Maine

## GO FROM "MAKE DO" TO "MAKE MORE"

Gene and Nedra learned that in Network Marketing, when you help enough people get what they want, you will get what you want. This fit perfectly with their core values, and they've never looked back.

We can't simply "make do" anymore, we have to "make more." That was the realization that Gene and Nedra came to in 1977, and it was humbling. Gene had a master's degree in software engineering and a great corporate job. Nedra, a college graduate herself, was a stay-at-home mom of three daughters. Gene took care of keeping a roof over their heads and trying to keep their car on the road. Nedra managed every savings strategy she could find, but it just wasn't enough. The car was falling apart, and there were no savings.

Two years earlier, Gene and their daughter, Thea, had been fighting colds and pneumonia all winter. Good friends Ruth and Jim suggested they try some nutritional supplements. Nedra resisted, saying vitamins don't work. Ruth told them, "Well, if they don't work, you'll get your money back."

Health results came quickly, and Nedra and Gene fell in love with the products. When Ruth and Jim encouraged them to take a look at the business, their decision to say yes came quickly. They knew they needed the extra income.

They began to talk to people, lots of people. They held in-home events, met people over coffee, and used lots of reach-out methods. Nedra talked with her sponsor, every day, realizing that a mentor coach can make the difference between success and discouragement. And, it worked.

In their first year, Nedra and Gene personally enrolled 40 people. In their second, they enrolled another 30, and began working down through the group. One of their first really successful leaders joined in year three. She was not a likely candidate for a business partner: 55 years old, eighth-grade education, and riddled with arthritis. No company would hire her.

The Sahrs watched their friend regain her health, earn her first new car, along with luxury vacations, and a $60,000 income. That became their tipping point. Helping others reach their dreams became a core value for Nedra and Gene.

They've been with the company now for 40 years. It's awarded them luxury trips all over the world. They've helped their three daughters through private undergraduate and graduate colleges. Nedra was able to complete her master's degree in nutrition with the idea of being of greater service to their team.

Today, Nedra and Gene live in a magical spot on the coast of Maine, are members of the company's Millionaire's Club, have over 15,000 member customers, and have a growing team of business partners who have made the decision to change their lives through helping others.

*This success story is not typical and is shared to inspire you and show you what's possible. It is not what you should expect to accomplish.*

# DeDe SHAW

Jensen Beach, Florida

## LEGACY OF LOVE

Successful international horse racing stable owners DeDe and George Shaw became highly decorated Network Marketers with a world-class lifestyle. DeDe is now continuing the legacy by expanding the organization she built with her late husband.

DeDe grew up working with horses. Her late husband, George Shaw, a talented businessman and professional harness racer, fit right in. "I knew from the beginning that if I were ever to date anybody, he had to be involved in horses," says DeDe.

DeDe and George teamed up and developed a highly profitable racing business. They had 100 client partnerships involved with them financially, so they knew about putting together a team. At that point, they had earned about $18 million in horse racing.

The Shaws found their company in the Yellow Pages. They had a horse that was unable to race because he was lame, and they were looking for anything that might help. "When I watched our horse walk soundly after we put him on the products, I was astonished," says DeDe. "Then later when we tried to take him off the products, he went lame. I knew we were on to something." (And, of course, DeDe and George enjoyed powerful product benefits for themselves.)

For five years the Shaws bought products at retail and never looked at the business. Then in 1981, they started searching for a franchise to purchase after retiring from horse racing. When they looked to the company with products that had performed so well for them, they saw a staggering potential for income, without the high level of risk or startup costs.

They hit the ground running. Their first month they sold $11,000 in products, just handing out catalogs in the mornings so they could be home with their son after school. They did meetings three nights a week, every week. George would focus on the income possibilities and DeDe would graciously share product stories. They would take "car loads" of people with them to meetings.

Within 22 months they had reached one of the highest ranks in their company and had helped 15 others achieve ranks as well. Within 36 months, they had reached the company's highest level. Today, the Shaw organization is the largest in their company. They have more than 500 leaders earning five- and six-figure incomes, and 50 teams that have also attained the company's highest rank.

When DeDe lost George in 2016, she discovered what an incredible legacy the two had created. They now have grandkids who are coming into the business. "We're sure glad we made the decision to join Network Marketing all those years ago," says DeDe. "We were able to be at home to raise our son and provide our family with substantial income, and now I am able to pass all that on to my grandchildren."

---

*This success story is not typical and is shared to inspire you and show you what's possible. It is not what you should expect to accomplish.*

# MARTY & SHERYL TURNER

Maplewood, Minnesota

## DON'T LET YOUR HISTORY KEEP YOU FROM YOUR DESTINY

When their first Network Marketing company suddenly went out of business, Marty and Sheryl were left shocked with no income. It took courage to start again, but now they're thriving with integrity and stability in their new home.

Raised by a single mother, Marty grew up on welfare. He was a hard worker, getting his first job at age 12 and buying his first car at age 15. He later became a competitive diver, and a locally and nationally ranked table tennis player. An entrepreneur at heart, Marty left college and started a successful software development company.

Sheryl chose networking so she could work from home after having three children in four years. She also co-owned a construction company and travel agency. After her 17-year marriage ended, she lost her house and had to make a home for her children in the basement of a commercial building. Later she bought a house. Ironically, her address was: 1 Inner Drive. With her youngest in college, she returned to the freedom of Network Marketing to rebuild her shattered life.

Marty and Sheryl's paths crossed when he answered an ad for a networking communication services company. They fell in love, got married, and built a massive organization of 28,000 partners. Unfortunately, the communications company went away. They were invited to look at the wellness industry by a friend from their prior company. Although Marty and Sheryl believed in the system, starting over was scary. They knew the challenge could either destroy them or move them forward.

They were dedicated to finding a solid company with integrity, stability, and organic products that people need and use every day. They wanted to create residual income, to build something they could leave to their three children and six grandchildren. They knew they wanted to be: Paid to Be Green.

At the time, Marty was working at his consulting business, and Sheryl at a bank. They built their networking business during lunch and after work. The first year they sponsored 22 partners. Two years later they had 7,000 partners and made more money in their part-time networking business than in their full-time jobs.

Marty and Sheryl reached the highest level in 32 months. They've earned many trips and bonuses, but it's the residual income that's been most vital …

When Sheryl was diagnosed with cancer, they were told to make final arrangements. Because of their residual income, Marty was able to focus entirely on helping Sheryl fight for her life, and they still got paid. Every month. Faith, family, and finances helped them fight for her life.

Today Sheryl is cancer-free. They have over 70,000 partners and travel the world, helping others create solid residual income and better health. They spend lots of time with their grandchildren, and they were able to care for Sheryl's mother when she was on hospice. Very few careers allow for that kind of time-luxury. No surprise they're so passionate about the profession of Network Marketing!

---

*This success story is not typical and is shared to inspire you and show you what's possible. It is not what you should expect to accomplish.*

# CAROLYN WIGHTMAN

Islamorada, Florida

## A CAREER WITH A CONSCIENCE

After being a Congressional staffer and a member of the Peace Corps in the South Pacific, Carolyn backed into becoming a Network Marketer. What began as sharing "eco-friendly" products became a life of freedom and a commitment to contribution and ongoing personal development.

With a prestigious college degree, and after spending a couple of years working inside Washington, D.C., Carolyn left for the first Peace Corps program in Polynesia. Her career challenge started when she came back to the U.S. with the classic question, "What's next?"

She knew what she did NOT want—being caged in a life on a schedule, with limits on rewards that someone else determined. She had no thoughts of being an entrepreneur, until …

When visiting her parents, helping them clean the house, her mom kept telling her: "You don't have to use so much. It's highly concentrated and doesn't pollute." This caught Carolyn's attention. She'd come back from untouched Polynesia to the stark contrast of smog and the mixed aromas of products in aerosol cans. People were just starting to think about the environment. She decided to track down the company that created the eco-friendly products her parents were using.

Carolyn started as a lot of people do. She first tested the products as a customer and gradually became passionate about the entire product line. She finally went to a meeting, and the more she listened to the speaker, the more it made sense.

The speaker had just qualified for a free car, earned some exotic trip, and was making twice as much in a month as Carolyn had made in Washington. She thought, "If that guy can do it, I can too." She had no idea how that one simple decision would impact her entire life.

Carolyn's first year was slow. She moved across the country (before the Internet), where she knew no one, so she essentially had to start over. By her third year, her organization started taking shape, and within four years, she was earning 5+ figures a month.

Today, with more than $5 million in sales a year, Carolyn runs her own schedule and travels when and where she wants. Her team of tens of thousands of people includes over 100 Pure Performance Olympians who have trained and medaled using the products she promotes.

She lives with her husband, "Captain Eddie," a career world-class fly fishing guide and entrepreneur in the Florida Keys. Their son grew up on the water, got his first passport when he was 2 weeks old, traveled the world with the family, and is now an entrepreneur on his own.

Having reached her company's highest rank, instead of "retiring," Carolyn's having too much fun. She maintains a passionate commitment to expanding her business with a purpose: creating a legacy and mentoring the next generation of entrepreneurs … in Partnership with Nature.

*This success story is not typical and is shared to inspire you and show you what's possible. It is not what you should expect to accomplish.*

# NOTES